The Little Princess

Philip M. Hudson

Copyright 2020 by Philip M. Hudson.

Published 2020.

Printed in the United States of America.

All rights reserved.

No portion of this book may be reproduced, stored in a retrieval system, or transmitted in any form or by any means - electronic, mechanical, photocopy, recording, scanning, or other - except for brief quotations in critical reviews or articles, without the prior written permission of the author.

ISBN 978-1-950647-52-1

Illustrations - Google Images.

This book may be ordered from online bookstores.

Publishing Services by BookCrafters
Parker, Colorado.
www.bookcrafters.net

Table of Contents

Prologue...i
Author's Note...xi
The Fairy Tale Begins...1
Epilogue..77

Appendix One – 100 Scriptures to Ponder...93
Appendix Two – List of Scriptures..301
About The Author...323
By The Author...325

Prologue

"Saturday's Warrior"

Lyrics by Doug Stewart

"Who
are these
children coming
down like gentle rain
thru darkened skies, with
glory trailing from their
feet as they go, and
endless promise in
their eyes?"

"Who are these young ones growing tall, growing strong, like silver trees against the storm; who will not bend with the wind or the change, but stand to fight the world alone?

"These are the few, the warriors saved for Saturday, to come the last day of the world. These are they, of Saturday. These are the strong, the warriors rising in their might to win the battle that is raging in the hearts of men, on Saturday."

viii

"Strangers from a realm of light, who have forgotten all; the memory of their former life and the purpose of their call. And so, they must learn why they're here, and who they really are."

Author's Note

For those who may be interested, two Appendices list one hundred scriptures that illustrate the familiarity of the prophets with our divine origin, as well as with our eternal destiny.

As you study them, they will strike resonant chords, not only if you are already familiar with the evocative doctrine of God's Plan of Happiness, but also if you are only now being introduced to the divine design He has created for us.

xvi

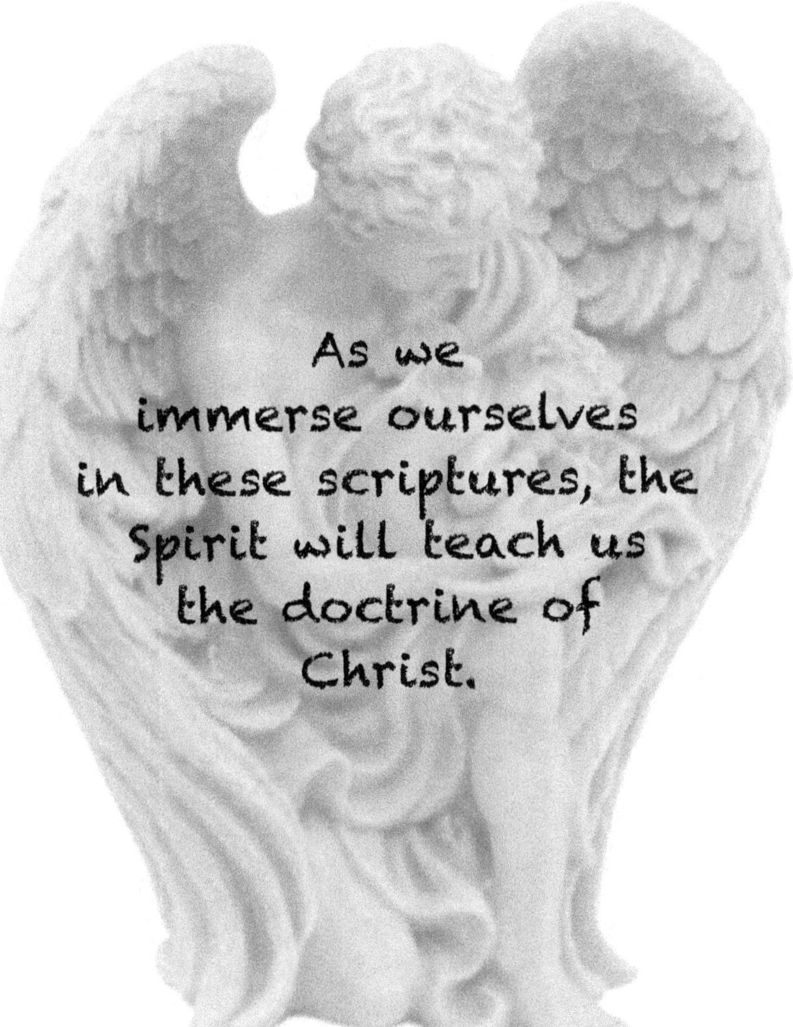

As we
immerse ourselves
in these scriptures, the
Spirit will teach us
the doctrine of
Christ.

That doctrine is the key to our discovery of eternal principles that can only be revealed by insight, intuition, and inspiration from the Holy Ghost.

xx

Our acceptance of that doctrine invites the Spirit to cast us off into streams of revelatory experiences that carry us along in the quickening currents of direct experience with our Father in Heaven.

As we walk in the light
and embrace true principles,
we will have charity toward others.
We will embrace the household of faith,
and virtue will continually garnish our
thoughts. Our confidence will swell
as the doctrine of the priesthood
distills upon our souls as the
dews from the heavens.

xxiv

The Holy Ghost
will bring to light the
true points of the doctrine
of Christ, that His Gospel might
be established, thereby to banish
confusion among those who
are seeking the truth.
(See D&C 10:62).

With the
Holy Ghost as our
constant companion, the
scepter of truth that we so
desperately need will become an
immutable staff of righteousness.
Our dominion will be everlasting,
and without compulsory means,
our return to the warm embrace
of our Father in our heavenly
home will become a
certain reality.

xxviii

The Fairytale Begins...

Once upon a time,
there was a little girl with
alabaster cheeks and ringlets
in her golden hair, who thought
she was about the luckiest child
on the face of the earth.

Her mommy and daddy loved her very much, and when she was in their presence, she felt deliciously warm, delightfully comfortable, and dazzlingly secure. The truth be told, she felt that she had been divinely blessed, although she would have been hard-put to explain to herself or to others her place in the cosmos.

Every morning, they would share their feelings and tell her they believed she was the most extraordinary little girl in the whole world. She even had a special name. They called her their "little princess."

They would cuddle her in their arms, give her a gentle squeeze, and ask: "How come you are such a delightful child?" And she would sheepishly reply, "I don't know. I think I just came this way."

She
did not know,
of course, where
she had really come
from, or why her bright
countenance scattered
sunshine wherever
she went.

Sometimes, they would ask her if she were sure that she was not a real princess? She would shrug her shoulders, not knowing if she really was a princess or not. In her heart of hearts, she was sure that it must be so, but these feelings also confused her, because she sensed the power of the unbreakable ties that had been forged between her and her mommy and daddy.

One crystal clear spring day, when the robins were hopping about on her front lawn in search of worms, and the daffodils in her mommy's flower garden were ready to burst out of their bulbs to shout salutations to the world, something even more remarkable happened.

An opportunity presented itself for her mommy and her daddy to discover why they had been so lucky to have a daughter such as theirs, and for all of them to find out, once and for all, if she really was a princess.

Two
young women
wearing black name
tags walked through their
front gate, made their way up
the flower-lined path to the
front porch, and knocked
expectantly on the
door.

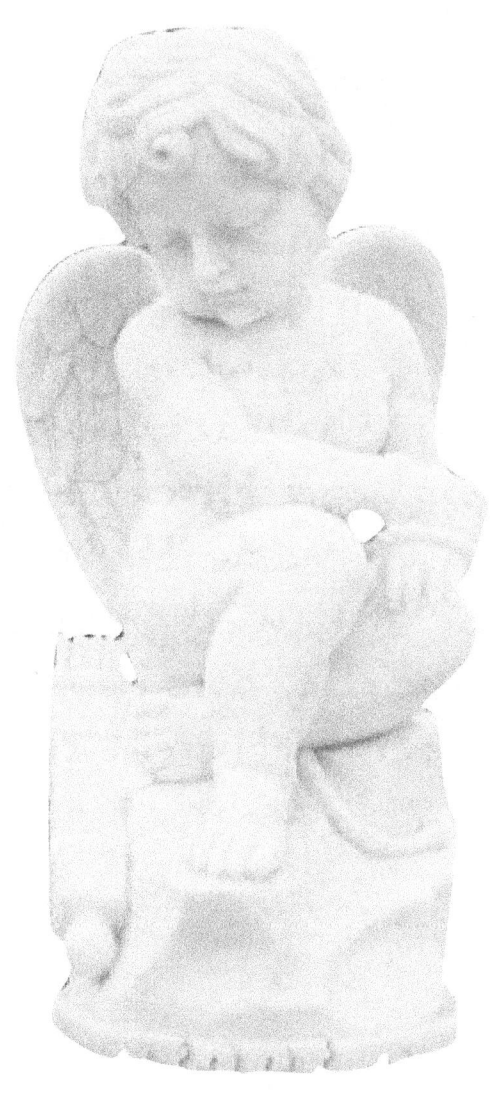

The family was impressed to greet them with warmth and hospitality, especially when, with glowing smiles on their faces, the young women introduced themselves as ambassadors of Jesus Christ.

The hairs on the back of the necks of the little girl's mommy and daddy tingled with an excitement that was as real as it was unexplainable.

Was it possible
that the Savior of
the world knew who
they were, and that He
had actually sent these
angels on His errand
to find them?

The young
women explained
how the Spirit of God
had, indeed, led them to
this particular home, where
they hoped that they might be
able to provide answers to life's
great questions, that, unbeknownst
to them, the family had been
pondering over the years.

The
thoughts that
had often perplexed
them related to where
they had come from, why
they were here on earth,
and where they were
going after their
life's journey
was over.

For
their family
was more important
to them than anything
else - more than gold
and silver, or any
of the cares of
the world.

Of course,
the little girl's
mommy and daddy
eagerly invited the two
young women into
their home.

The visit that followed was magical. There was an electricity in the air, and to everyone present, it seemed as if time itself stood still.

As had the travelers on the Road to Emmaus, who supped with the Savior of the world, the mommy and daddy thought to themselves: "Have not our hearts burned within us, while they have talked with us by the way, and while they have opened to us the scriptures?" (See Luke 24:32).

The young ladies were able to answer all of their questions. These included many that the family had never before thought to ask!

The little girl's mommy and daddy were shown how they could trace their family tree, not with their fingers, but with their hearts, and in doing so, they made a most wonderful discovery.

They
learned that their
precious daughter was a
very important member of a
royal household, and that, in
a real sense, she had another
Father and Mother who were
the King and Queen
of Heaven.

Still, the
little girl wanted
to remain a part of
the only family that she
had ever known, and that
she had grown to love
even more than life
itself.

But, all
was made right, as
the family was taught yet
another glorious truth. She
was her mommy and daddy's
daughter, too, and God had
a Plan that would make it
possible for their family
to be knit together
forever!

She could be with her parents, and they with her, and Heavenly Father would be reunited with His children. They would no longer be "strangers and foreigners, but fellow citizens with the Saints, and of the household of God." (Ephesians 2:19).

The young women who
visited with the family explained
that their daughter had come to her
earthly parents from their Father in
Heaven, Who loved her very much,
and Who wanted her to find
happiness through faith in
Jesus Christ, while she
lived on the earth.

Thru His "Saviors
on Mount Zion," He would
introduce her to the household
rules that she would need to learn
and to obey while here, that she might
qualify by worthiness to return with
nobility to her Father in Heaven
after her earth life was over.

Therefore,
God had made sure
that when she left His
kingdom, she would come
to her new home on earth,
where her mommy and her
daddy had been praying
to Him, that He might
bless them with
a child.

The missionaries described this Plan as God's "Divine Design for Happiness," which struck a familiar chord and made perfect sense to the family.

They felt as if
they were being taught
things that they already
knew, but that had been
lying dormant, in the
recesses of memory,
awaiting only a
quickening by
the Spirit.

The young women described as 'religious recognition' the feelings that the family was experiencing, and explained that when Gospel principles are introduced to earnest seekers of the truth, they are accompanied by the independent witness of the Holy Ghost.

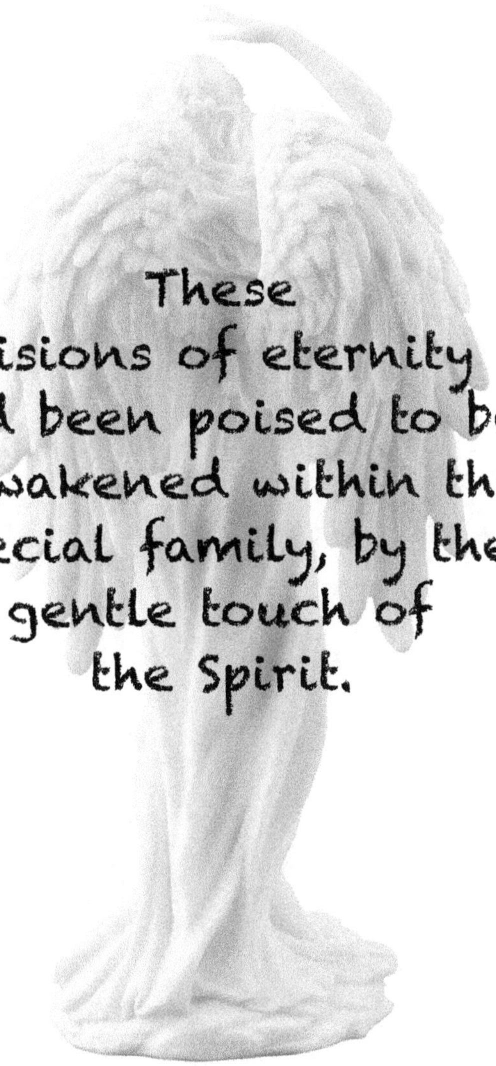

These
visions of eternity
had been poised to be
reawakened within this
special family, by the
gentle touch of
the Spirit.

Our Father
in Heaven knew
the hearts of the little
girl's mommy and daddy,
for He is the Master Potter. He
created them, and they were
as pliable clay in His
hands.

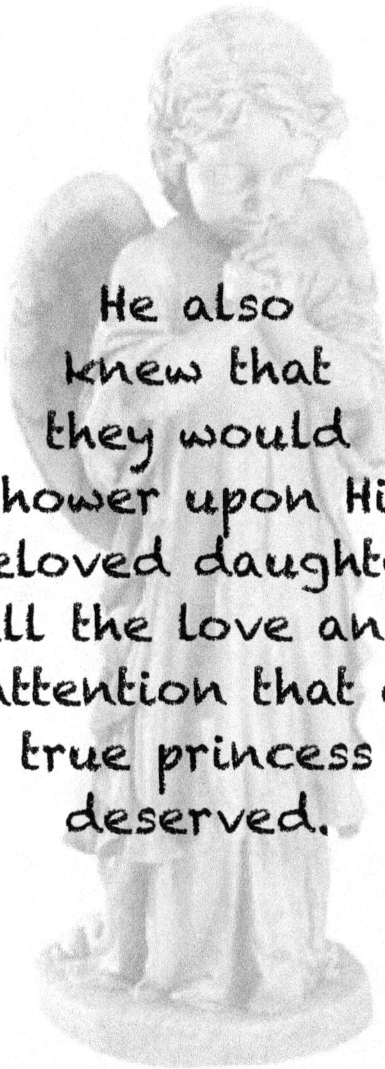

He also
knew that
they would
shower upon His
beloved daughter
all the love and
attention that a
true princess
deserved.

As they learned more about the Gospel of Jesus Christ, she and her family began to understand more deeply the meaning of the expression "heaven on earth."

The little
girl and her
mommy and daddy
were now prepared to
move forward, for they all
understood more clearly that,
although they had miles to go
before they slept, there were
promises to God that
must yet be kept.

They
had been blessed
with the knowledge of
who they really were; that
the "little princess" belonged
not only to her mommy and her
daddy, but also to the King and
Queen who rule and reign over
all things bright and beautiful,
and all creatures great and
small, from the heavens
above.

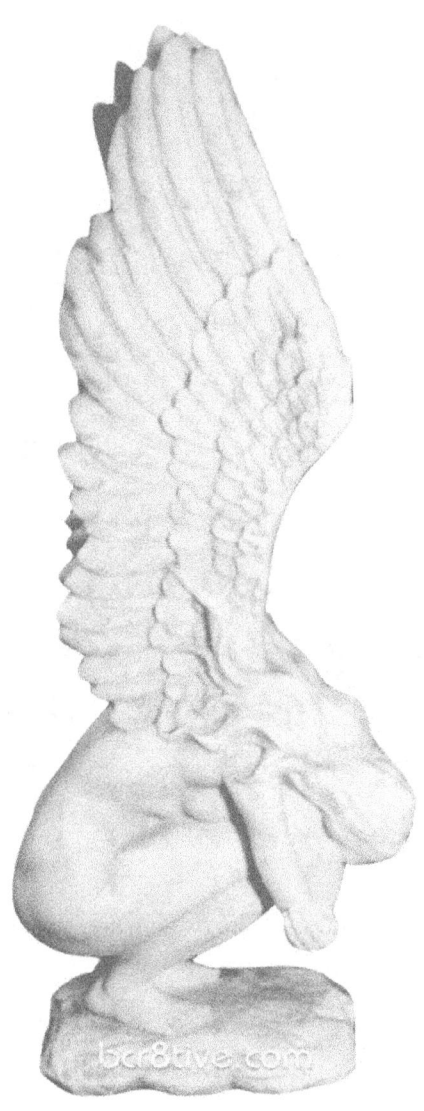

With
the additional
example provided by
Jesus Christ, and through
the miracle of His Atonement,
they were able to envision God's
Great Plan of Salvation, and how
it could bless them through His
heavenly grace to enjoy their
righteous inheritance amid
celestial glories.

And so, as in the best of fairy tales, they all lived happily ever after, even for time and for all of eternity.

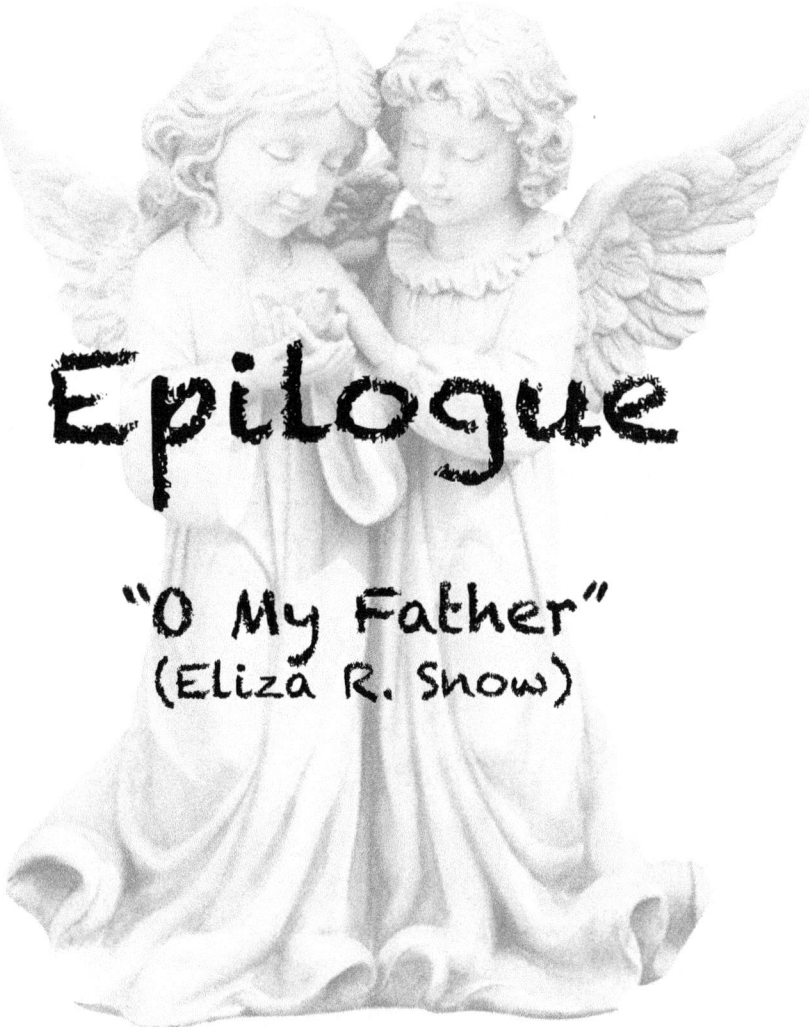

Epilogue

"O My Father"
(Eliza R. Snow)

"O my Father, Thou that dwellest in the high and glorious place, when shall I regain Thy presence, and again behold Thy face? In Thy holy habitation, did my spirit once reside? In my first primeval childhood, was I nurtured near Thy side?"

"For a wise and glorious purpose, Thou hast placed me here on earth, and withheld the recollection of my former friends and birth."

"Yet, oft-times a secret something whispered: 'You're a stranger here,' and I felt that I had wandered from a more exalted sphere."

"I had learned to call Thee Father, thru Thy Spirit from on high. But, until the key of knowledge was restored, I knew not why."

"In the
heavens are
parents single?
No, the thought
makes reason stare!
Truth is reason, truth
eternal tells me
I've a Mother
there."

88

"When I leave this frail existence, when I lay this mortal by, Father, Mother, may I meet You in Your royal courts on high?"

"Then, at length, when I've completed all you sent me forth to do, with Your mutual approbation, let me come and dwell with You."

"Our birth is but a
sleep and a forgetting.
The soul that rises with us,
our life's star, hath had elsewhere
its setting, and cometh from afar.
Not in entire forgetfulness, and not
in utter nakedness, but trailing
clouds of glory do we come
from God, Who is our
Home." (Wordsworth).

Appendix One

100 scriptures to ponder, that relate to our premortal relationship with our Heavenly Father.

Old Testament

Moses shared wonderful news with all of Israel: "Ye are the children of the Lord your God" (Deuteronomy 14:1).

He asked them
to "remember the days of old,
when the most High divided to the
nations their inheritance; when he
separated the sons of Adam, he
set the bounds of the people
according to the number of
the children of Israel."
(Deuteronomy 32:7-8).

"And they fell upon their faces, and said, O God, the God of the spirits of all flesh." (Numbers 16:22).

"Let the Lord, the God of the spirits of all flesh, set a man over the congregation." (Numbers 27:16).

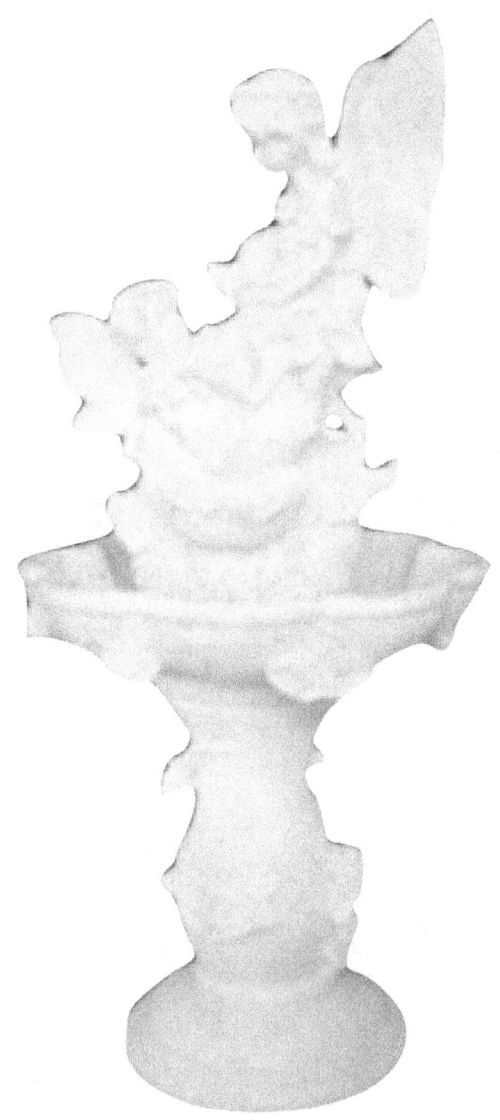

"God the Lord ... created the heavens, and stretched them out; he ... spread forth the earth, and that which cometh out of it; he ... giveth breath unto the people upon it, and spirit to them that walk therein." (Isaiah 42:5).

"Before
I formed
thee in the belly
I knew thee; and
before thou camest
forth out of the womb
I sanctified thee."
(Jeremiah 1:5).

"There was a day when the sons of God came to present themselves before the Lord, and Satan came also among them to present himself before the Lord." (Job 2:1).

"Where wast thou when I laid the foundations of the earth? Declare, if thou hast understanding. Who hath laid the measures thereof, if thou knowest, or who hath stretched the line upon it?" (Job 38:4-5).

"Whereupon are the foundations thereof fastened, or who laid the corner stone thereof, when the morning stars sang together, and all the sons of God shouted for joy?" (Job 38:6-7).

"The Lord
hath said unto me,
Thou art my son."
(Psalms 2:7).

"All of you
are children
of the most High."
(Psalms 82:6).

"The Lord possessed me in the beginning of his way, before his works of old. I was set up from everlasting, from the beginning, or ever the earth was. When there were no depths, I was brought forth; when there were no fountains abounding with water."
(Proverbs 8:22-24).

"Before the
mountains were settled,
before the hills was I brought
forth. While as yet he had not made
the earth, nor the fields, nor the highest
part of the dust of the world. When he
prepared the heavens, I was there;
when he set a compass upon
the face of the depth."
(Proverbs 8:25-27).

"When he established the clouds above, (and) when he strengthened the fountains of the deep; when he gave to the sea his decree, that the waters should not pass his commandment; when he appointed the foundations of the earth. Then, I was by him, as one brought up with him, and I was daily his delight, rejoicing always before him." (Proverbs 8:28-30).

After the conlusion of our mortal lives "shall the dust return to the earth as it was, and the spirit shall return unto God who gave it." (Ecclesiastes 12:7).

The inspiring words of prophets of old are true. We "are the sons (and daughters) of the living God" (Hosea 1:10).

"The burden of the word of the Lord for Israel, saith the Lord, which stretcheth forth the heavens, and layeth the foundation of the earth, and formeth the spirit of man within him." (Zechariah 12:1).

Within our
beating hearts
is a yearning to
know: "Have we not
all one father?"
(Malachi 2:10).

"Hath not one God created us? (Malachi 2:10).

New Testament

"Blessed are the peacemakers:
for they shall be called
the children of God."
(Matthew 5:9).

We are "the children of (our) Father which is in heaven, (Who) maketh his sun to rise on the evil and on the good, and sendeth rain on the just and on the unjust." (Matthew 5:45).

"Be ye therefore perfect, even as your Father which is in heaven is perfect." (Matthew 5:48).

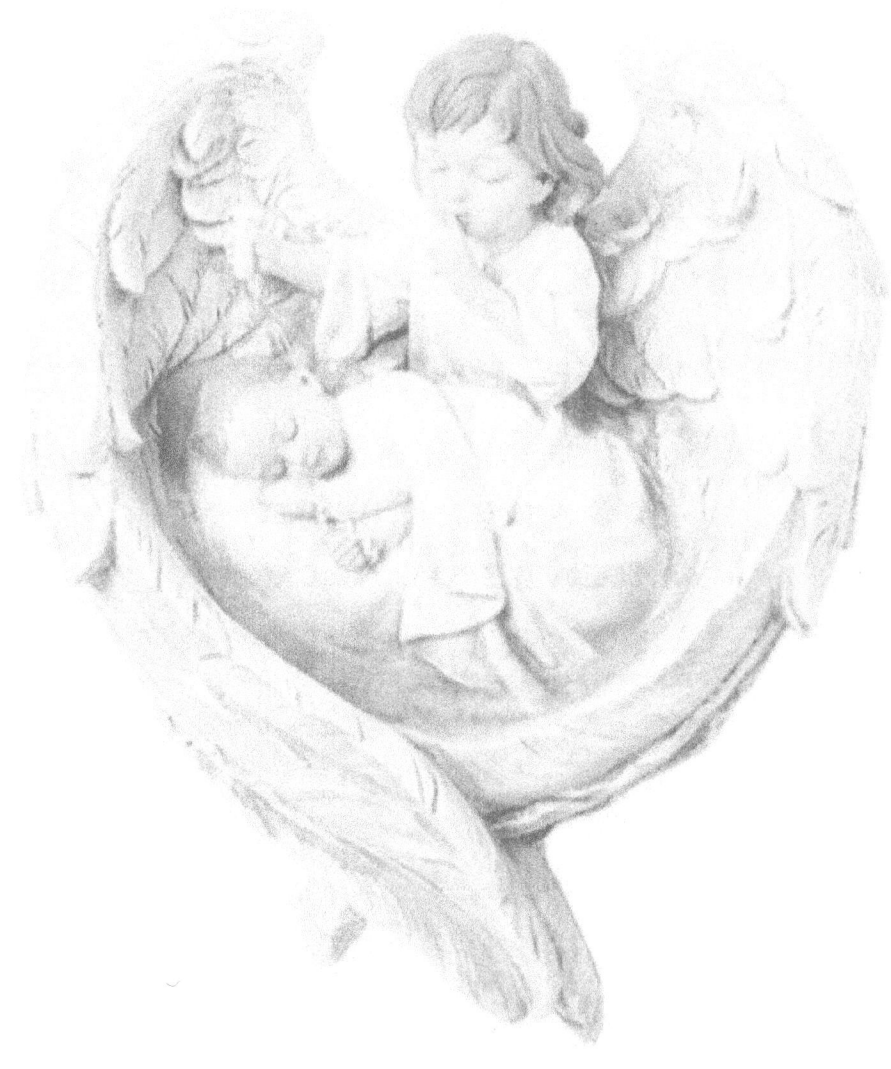

"Call no man your father upon the earth: for one is your Father, which is in heaven." (Matthew 23:9).

"From the beginning of creation, God made (us) male and female." (Mark 10:6).

"Let us alone.
What have we to do with
thee, thou Jesus of Nazareth?
Art thou come to destroy us?
I know thee, who thou art,
the Holy One of God."
(Luke 4:34).

"They are equal unto the angels, and are the children of God." (Luke 20:36).

"Jesus knew from the beginning who they were that believed not, and who should betray him." (John 6:64).

"Ye shall also bear witness, because ye have been with me from the beginning." (John 15:27).

Our Father "hath made of one blood all nations for to dwell on all the face of the earth, and hath determined the times before appointed, and the bounds of their habitation." (Acts 17:26).

Luke
understood that in
our Heavenly Father,
"we live, and move, and
have our being, as certain
also of your own poets
have said. For we are
also his offspring."
(Acts 17:28).

"We are the offspring of God." (Acts 17:29).

"For as many as are led by the Spirit of God, they are the sons of God." (Romans 8:14).

"The Spirit itself beareth witness with our spirit, that we are the children of God. And if children, then heirs ... of God." (Romans 8:16).

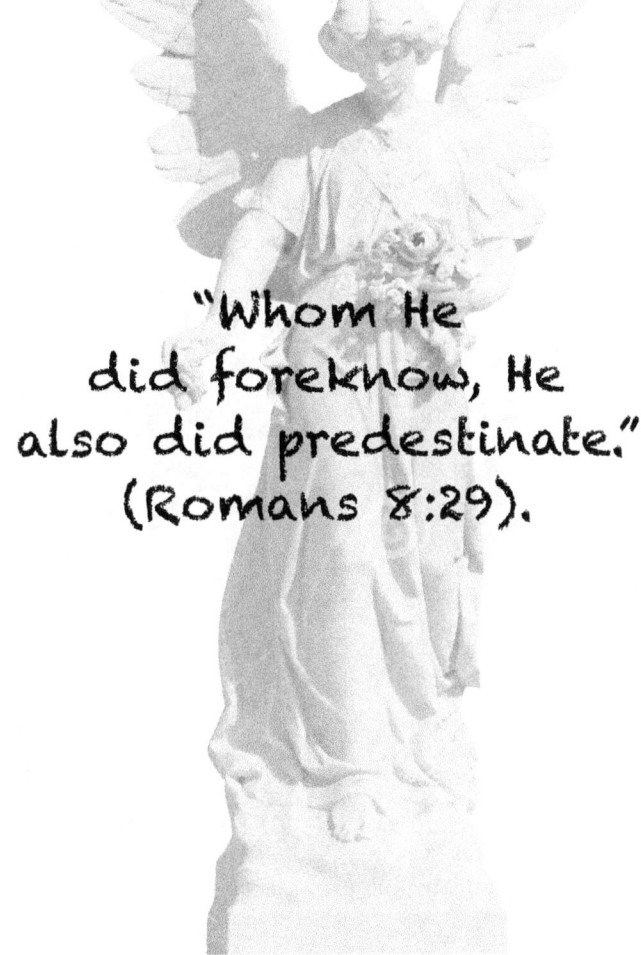

"Whom He did foreknow, He also did predestinate." (Romans 8:29).

"They which are the children of the flesh, these are not the children of God: but the children of the promise are counted for the seed." (Romans 9:8).

"There shall they be called the children of the living God." (Romans 9:26).

"Ye are all the children of God by faith in Christ Jesus." (Galatians 3:26).

"The natural man receiveth not the things of the Spirit of God, for they are foolishness unto him; neither can he know them, because they are spiritually discerned." But those who are willing to open themselves up to possibilities they had never before considered "have the mind of Christ." (1 Corinthians 2:14 & 16).

"To us, there is but one God, the Father, of whom are all things, we in him." (1 Corinthians 8:6).

"Ye shall be my sons and daughters." (2 Corinthians 6:18).

Ye are "blameless and harmless, the sons of God, without rebuke, in the midst of a crooked and perverse nation, among whom ye shine as lights in the world." (Philippians 2:15).

182

"Blessed be the God
and Father of our Lord
Jesus Christ ... according as
he hath chosen us in him before
the foundation of the world, that
we should be holy and without
blame before him in love."
(Ephesians 1:3-4).

Heavenly Father
"predestinated us unto
the adoption of children
by Jesus Christ to himself,
according to the good
pleasure of his will."
(Ephesians 1:5).

"Ye are no more strangers and foreigners, but fellowcitizens with the saints, and of the household of God." (Ephesians 2:19).

"For this cause,
I bow my knees unto the
Father of our Lord Jesus Christ,
of whom the whole family in
heaven and earth is named."
(Ephesians 3:14-15).

The declaration rings loud and clear, as it resonates within our breasts. He is "the Father of all." (Ephesians 4:6).

"Till we all come in the unity of the faith, and of the knowledge of the Son of God, unto a perfect man, unto the measure of the stature of the fulness of Christ." (Ephesians 4:13).

"Be ye therefore followers of God, as dear children." (Ephesians 5:1).

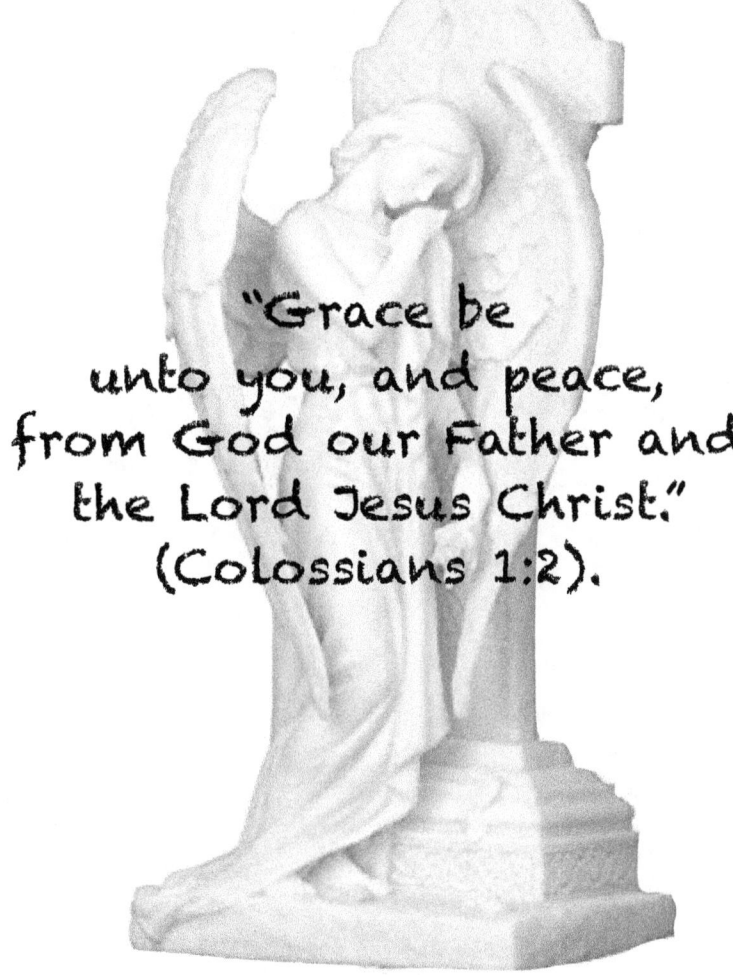

"Grace be unto you, and peace, from God our Father and the Lord Jesus Christ." (Colossians 1:2).

"God hath from the beginning chosen you to salvation through santification of the Spirit and belief on the truth." (2 Thessalonians 2:13).

"Our Lord Jesus Christ himself, and God, even our Father ... hath loved us." (2 Thessalonians 2:16).

"God
"hath saved us,
and called us with an
holy calling, not according
to our works, but according to
his own purpose and grace, which
was given us in Christ Jesus
before the world began."
(2 Timothy 1:8).

Those who kept their first estate now live "in the hope of eternal life, which God, that cannot lie, promised (to each of His children) before the world began, according to the promise of life which is in Christ Jesus." (Titus 1:2 & 2 Timothy 1:1).

"Thou art my son. This day I have begotten thee. And ... I will be to (you) a Father, and (you) shall be to me a son." (Hebrews 1:5).

"Furthermore, we have had fathers of our flesh which corrected us, and we gave them reverence. Shall we not much rather be in subjection unto the Father of spirits, and live?" (Hebrews 12:9).

We are "elect according to the foreknowledge of God the Father." (1 Peter 1:2).

"Behold, what manner of love the Father hath bestowed upon us, that we should be called the sons of God." (1 John 3:1).

"Beloved, now are we the sons of God, and it doth not yet appear what we shall be: but we know that, when he shall appear, we shall be like him; for we shall see him as he is."
(1 John 3:2).

"By this we know that we love the children of God, when we love God, and keep his commandments."
(1 John 5:2).

"The angels which kept not their first estate, but left their own habitation, he hath reserved in everlasting chains under darkness unto the judgment of the great day." (Jude 1:6).

Book of Mormon

"The Lord hath created the earth that it should be inhabited, and he hath created his children that they should possess it." (1 Nephi 17:36).

"God is "the Father of heaven and earth, the Creator of all things from the beginning." (Mosiah 3:8).

"All mankind, yea, men and women, all nations, kindreds, tongues and people, must be born again; yea, born of God, changed from their carnal and fallen state to a state of righteousness, being redeemed of God, becoming (once again) his sons and daughters." (Mosiah 27:25-26).

"And this is the manner after which they were ordained – being called and prepared from the foundation of the world according to the foreknowledge of God."
(Alma 13:3).

"It has been made known unto me by an angel, that the spirits of all men, as soon as they are departed from this mortal body, yea, the spirits of all men, whether they be good or evil, are taken home to that God who gave them life."
(Alma 40:11).

"The resurrection of Christ redeemeth mankind ... and bringeth them back into the presence of the Lord." (Helaman 14:17, see also Mormon 9:13, Alma 42:23, & Ether 3:13).

Doctrine & Covenants

"Behold, thou art Hyrum, my son. Seek the kingdom of God, and all things shall be added according to thst which is just."
(D&C 11:23)

The Lord told Joseph Smith how the creative process has taken place: "By the power of my Spirit created I them; yea, all things both spiritual and temporal; First spiritual, secondly temporal." (D&C 29:31-32).

240

It is the destiny of the earth to "be filled with the measure of man, according to his creation before the world was made."
(D&C 49:17).

242

"By Him, and thru him, and of him, the worlds are and were created, and the inhabitants thereof are begotten sons and daughters unto God." (D&C 76:24).

"Wherefore, as it is written, they are gods, even the sons of God." (D&C 76:58).

246

"That which is spiritual (is) in the likeness of that which is temporal; and that which is temporal is in the likeness of that which is spiritual; the spirit of man in the likeness of his person." (D&C 77:2).

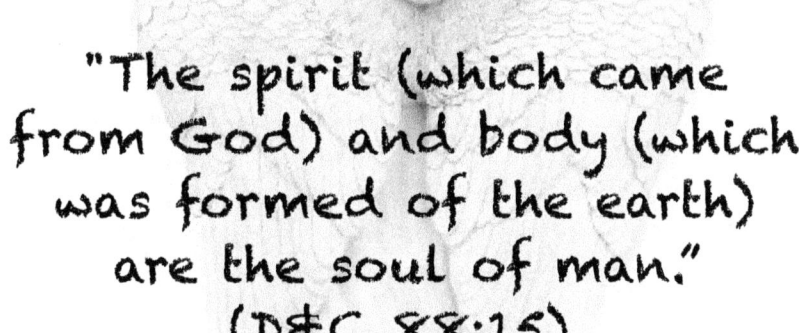

"The spirit (which came from God) and body (which was formed of the earth) are the soul of man." (D&C 88:15).

"I was in the beginning with the Father, and am the Firstborn. Ye were also in the beginning with the Father." (D&C 93:21 & 23).

"Man was also in the beginning with God." (D&C 93:29).

"For man is spirit, the elements are eternal, and spirit and element, inseparably connected, receive a fullness of joy." (D&C 93:33).

"Every spirit of man was innocent in the beginning." (D&C 93:38).

"I was ordained from before the foundation of the world." (D&C 127:2).

"There is
a law, irrevocably
decreed in heaven before
the foundation of the world."
(D&C 130:2).

262

"Joseph, my son ... trouble me no more on this matter." (D&C 130:15).

"All
who will
have a blessing
at my hands shall
abide the law which was
appointed for that blessing,
and the conditions thereof,
as were instituted from
before the foundation
of the world."
(D&C 132:5).

"Before
they were born,
they, with many others,
received their first lessons
in the world of spirits and were
prepared to come forth in the due
time of the Lord to labor in his
vineyard for the salvation
of the souls of men."
(D&C 138:56).

Pearl of Great Price

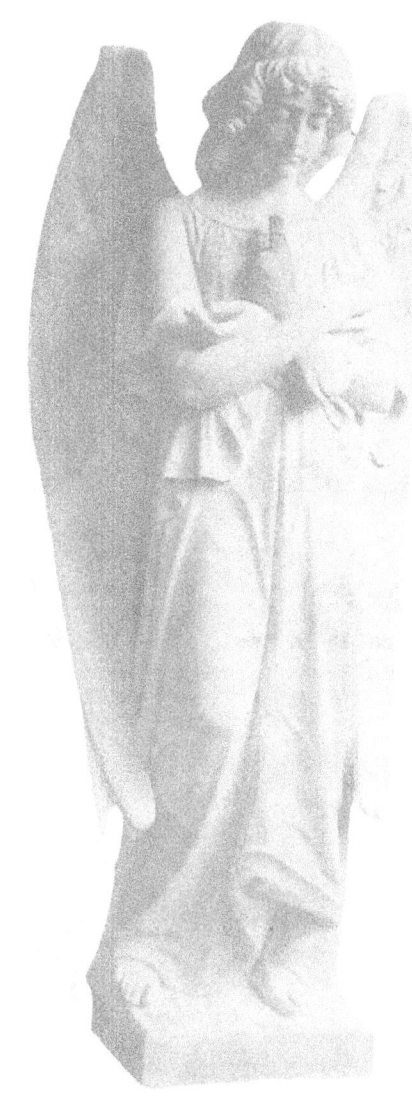

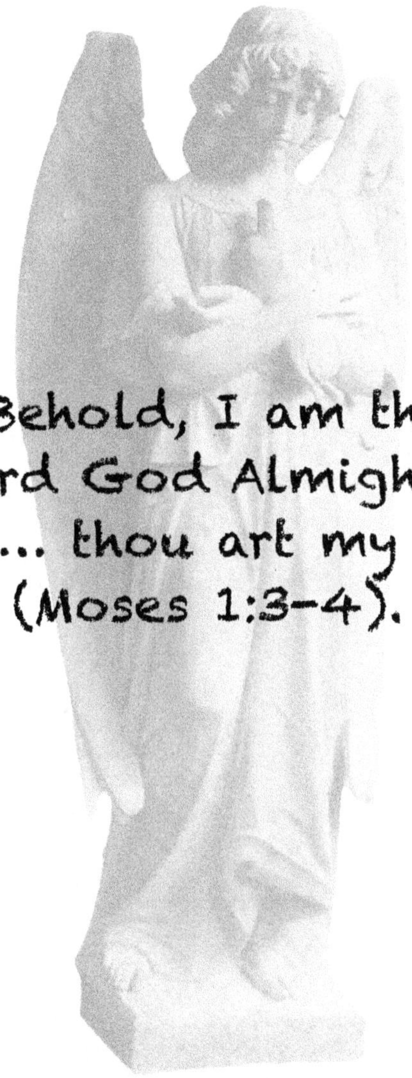

"Behold, I am the
Lord God Almighty,
and ... thou art my son."
(Moses 1:3-4).

"I have a work for thee, Moses, my son; and thou art in the similitude of mine Only Begotten." (Moses 1:6-7).

"And it came to pass that Moses looked upon Satan and said: Who art thou? For behold, I am a son of God, in the similitude of his Only Begotten; and where is thy glory, that I should worship thee?" (Moses 1:13).

"I, the Lord God, created all things ... spiritually, before they were naturally upon the face of the earth." (Moses 3:5).

"Now this prophecy Adam spake, as he was moved upon by the Holy Ghost, and a genealogy was kept of the children of God. And this was the book of the generations of Adam, saying: In the day that God created man, in the likeness of God made he him."
(Moses 6:8).

"And this is the genealogy of the sons of Adam, who was the son of God, with whom God, himself, conversed." (Moses 6:22).

Enoch "beheld the spirits that God had created, and he beheld also things which were not visible to the natural eye." (Moses 6:36).

Scriptural insight stirs our spirits and confirms the truth: "I am God," the Lord told Moses. "I made the world, and all men before they were in the flesh." (Moses 6:51).

"Thou art one in me,
a son of God."
(Moses 6:68).

"Unto thy brethren have I said, and also given commandment, that they should love one another, and that they should choose me, their Father." (Moses 7:33).

"Noah and his sons hearkened unto the Lord, and gave heed, and they were called the sons of God." (Moses 8:13).

"The right belonging to the fathers ... was conferred upon me from the fathers; it came down from the fathers, from the beginning of time, yea, even from the beginning, or before the foundation of the earth, down to the present time."
(Abraham 1:2–3).

"Now the Lord had shown unto me, Abraham, the intelligences that were organized before the world was, and among all these there were many of the noble and great ones." (Abraham 3:22).

"We will go down, for there is space there, and we will take of these materials, and we will make an earth whereon these may dwell; and we will prove them herewith, to see if they will do all things whatsoever the Lord their God shall command them." (Abraham 3:24-25).

"They who keep their first estate shall be added upon ... and they who keep their second estate shall have glory added upon their heads for ever and ever." (Abraham 3:26).

"The Gods formed man from the dust of the ground, and took his spirit (that is, the man's spirit), and put it into him; and breathed into his nostrils the breath of life, and man became a living soul." (Abraham 5:7).

Appendix Two

100 scripture references in the order in which they appear in Appendix One.

Old Testament

19

Deuteronomy 14:1
Deuteronomy 32:7-8
Numbers 16:22
Numbers 27:16
Isaiah 42:5
Jeremiah 1:5
Job 2:1
Job 38:4-5
Job 38:6-7
Psalms 2:7
Psalms 82:6
Proverbs 8:22-24
Proverbs 8:25-27
Proverbs 8:28-30
Ecclesiastes 12:7
Hosea 1:10
Zechariah 12:1
Malachi 2:10
Malachi 2:10

308

New Testament

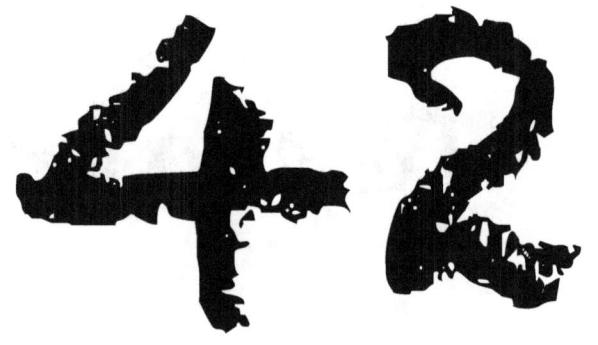

Matthew 5:9
Matthew 5:45
Matthew 5:48
Matthew 6:9
Matthew 23:9
Mark 10:6
Luke 4:34
Luke 20:36
John 6:64
John 15:27
Acts 17:26
Acts 17:28
Acts 17:29
Romans 8:14
Romans 8:16
Romans 8:29
Romans 9:8
Romans 9:26
Galatians 3:26
1 Corinthians 2:14 & 16
1 Corinthians 8:6

2 Corinthians 6:18
Philippians 2:15
Ephesians 1:3-4
Ephesians 1:5
Ephesians 2:19
Ephesians 3:14-15
Ephesians 4:6
Ephesians 4:13
Ephesians 5:1
Colossians 1:2
2 Thessalonians 2:13
2 Thessalonians 2:16
2 Timothy 1:8
Titus 1:2 & 2 Timothy 1:1
Hebrews 1:5
Hebrews 12:9
1 Peter 1:2
1 John 3:1
1 John 3:2
1 John 5:2
Jude 1:6

Book of Mormon

1 Nephi 17:36 Alma 13:3
Mosiah 3:8 Alma 40:11
Mosiah 27:25-26 Helaman 14:17

Doctrine & Covenants

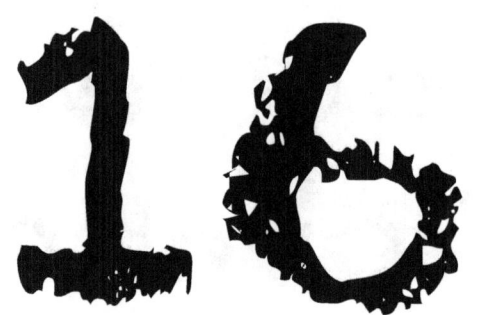

D&C 11:23
D&C 29:31-32
D&C 49:17
D&C 76:24
D&C 76:58
D&C 77:2
D&C 88:15
D&C 93:21 & 23

D&C 93:29
D&C 93:33
D&C 93:38
D&C 127:2
D&C 130:2
D&C 130:15
D&C 132:5
D&C 138:56

Pearl of Great Price

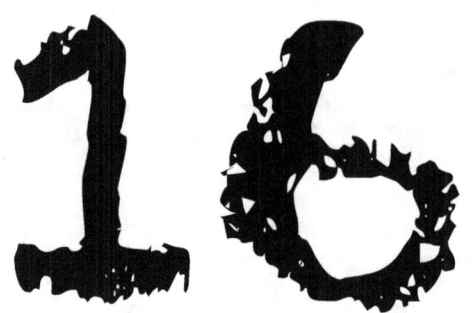

Moses 1:3-4	Moses 6:68
Moses 1:6-7	Moses 7:33
Moses 1:13	Moses 8:13
Moses 3:5	Abraham 1:2-3
Moses 6:8	Abraham 3:22
Moses 6:22	Abraham 3:24-25
Moses 6:36	Abraham 3:26
Moses 6:51	Abraham 5:7

About The Author

Phil Hudson and his wife Jan have 7 children and over 25 grandchildren. They enjoy spending time with their family at their cabin nestled in the Selkirk Mountains, on the shore of Priest Lake, the crown jewel of North Idaho. Phil had a successful dental practice in Spokane, Washington for 43 years, before retiring in 2015. He has an eclectic mix of hobbies, and enjoys the out of doors. He always finds time, however, to record his thoughts on his laptop, and understands Isaac Asimov's response when he was asked: If you knew that you had only 10 minutes left to live, what would you do?" He answered: "I'd type faster."

Phil received the inspiration to write this book while he and Jan were serving as missionaries for The Church of Jesus Christ of Latter-day Saints, in the Kingdom of Tonga. While there, they celebrated their 50th wedding anniversary.

By The Author

Essays

    Volume One: Spray From The Ocean Of Thought
    Volume Two: Ripples On A Pond
    Volume Three: Serendipitous Meanderings
    Volume Four: Presents Of Mind
    Volume Five: Mental Floss
    Volume Six: Fitness Training For The Mind And Spirit

First Principles and Ordinances Series

    Faith - Our Hearts Are Changed
    Repentance - A Broken Heart and a Contrite Spirit
    Baptism - One Hundred And One Reasons Why We Are Baptized
    The Holy Ghost - That We Might Have His Spirit To Be With Us
    The Sacrament - This Do In Remembrance Of Me

Book of Mormon Commentary

    Volume One: Born In The Wilderness
    Volume Two: Voices From The Dust
    Volume Three: Journey To Cumorah

Doctrine & Covenants Commentary

    Volume One - Sections 1 - 34
    Volume Two - Sections 35 - 57

Minute Musings: Spontaneous Combustions of Thought

    Volume One
    Volume Two
    Volume Three

Calendars:

    As I Think About The Savior
    In His Own Words: Discovering William Tyndale
    Scriptural Symbols

Children & Youth

    Book of Mormon Hiking Song
    Happy Birthday
    Muddy, Muddy
    The Hiawatha Trail: An Allegory
    The Little Princess
    The Parable of The Pencil
    The Thirteen Articles of Faith

Doctrinal Themes

- Are Christians Mormon? Volume One
- Are Christians Mormon? Volume One
- Christmas is The Season When...
- Dentistry in The Scriptures
- Gratitude
- Hebrew Poetry
- Hiding in Plain Sight
- One Hundred Questions Answered by The Book of Mormon
- The Highways and Byways of Life
- The House of The Lord
- The Parable of The Pencil
- Without The Book of Mormon
- Writing on Metal Plates

A Thought For Each Day of the Year

- Baptism
- Faith
- Life's Greatest Questions
- Repentance
- Revelation
- The Atonement
- The Holy Ghost
- The House of the Lord
- The Plan of Salvation
- The Sabbath
- The Sacrament

Professional Publications

- Diode Laser Soft Tissue Surgery Volume One
- Diode Laser Soft Tissue Surgery Volume Two
- Diode Laser Soft Tissue Surgery Volume Three

These, and other titles, are available from online retailers.

Quid magis possum dicere?

www.ingramcontent.com/pod-product-compliance
Lightning Source LLC
Chambersburg PA
CBHW060507240426
43661CB00007B/944